Celebrating the A4s

Images from the Transport Treasury archive
Compiled by Hector Maxwell

© Images and design: Transport Treasury 2024 Text: Hector Maxwell

ISBN 978-1-913893-17-0

First published in 2024 by Transport Treasury Publishing Limited. 16 Highworth Close, High Wycombe, HP13 7PJ.
Totem Publishing an imprint of Transport Treasury Publishing.

www.ttpublishing.co.uk

Printed in Tarxien, Malta by Gutenberg Press Ltd.

'*Celebrating the A4s*' is one of many books on specialist transport subjects published in strictly limited numbers and
produced under the Totem Publishing imprint using material only available at The Transport Treasury.

Front Cover: No 60016 *Silver King* in grimy condition leaving Kings Cross with the down 'Norseman' service. Contrary to what might otherwise be the first impression, this was not a service to East Anglia, but instead a Newcastle train direct to Newcastle for Tyne Commission Quay to connect with the ferry service to Norway.

Frontispiece: The classic image of an 'A4'. This is No 60003 the renamed *Andrew K McCosh* on Holloway bank with the down 9.40am to Newcastle.

Rear Cover: Journeys end; Kings Cross. A timeless piece featuring Nos 60034 *Lord Faringdon* and 60022 *Mallard*. (*George Heiron*)

Introduction

So where does one start on a new book on the A4s? 'Weight for weight' probably more film has been expended on these 34 engines (I appreciate there had originally been 35 but one was destroyed in WW2) than probably any other comparative class and as time passes ever more views come to the surface. The Transport Treasury archive is an example of this, most of the named collections contains at least a few views of the class whilst filed separately considerable drawer space is taken up with class members: and that is before we start digging in other corners as well!

So why from a Southern man is there a fascination with A4s? Two reasons really, the first is that from photographs, I personally think a clean A4 in BR green – without the valances (side skirts according to Mr Yeadon), was a joy to the eyes. Perhaps even more so was back in the 1960s, when the class were on their last workings on the East Coast main line, I was fortunate enough to see one in full flight complete with chime whistle sounding. I doubt if I was more than 10 or 12 at the time; whilst trying to analyse how this had happened I seem to recall being taken for a visit to 'A.N. Other' somewhere alongside the main line out of Kings Cross. I recall it was a bright sunny morning and the railway was on an embankment behind where we were visiting.

I was well used to the Bulleid and Stanier whistles, even the Great Western and occasional LMS hoot – the latter more like the sound of the Isle of Wight ferry to me, but suddenly the quietness of the morning air was rent asunder by something I had never heard before. Turning I was able to witness a beautifully clean engine with steam pouring back from the chimney and whistle. Seen sideways-on it presented a sight I can still visualise decades later. I have no recollection of the train behind, or for that matter and as stated above, who we saw and why. Such things were insignificant, I had seen my first and (as it turned out to be) only A4 in steam in BR service).

So enough of the romanticism. Why the liking for the design? Simply put I think it 'looks right'. I recall reading years ago that if something, looks right it is right and certainly from an observer's perspective that law applies. The purist may say, 'No, they were far better with the fairing...', or 'LNER blue (or silver) was better'. I would disagree. To me the fairings made the engine appear dated, but from ground level – or as it turned out – embankment level – the characteristic lines of Sir Nigel Gresley's design (or was it Mr Bulleid who was responsible for the external styling?) were just about right.

No 60001

No 60001 *Sir Ronald Matthews*, named after the Chairman of the LNER at the time, at Gateshead shed and in company with another member of the class, No 60020, in the background. Both engines are coaled ready for their next duty. At the front the 'cods mouth' has been opened; both top and bottom portions opened simultaneously; this was accomplished by the use of winding key inserted into the side frame. The idea for this came from an un-named Doncaster draughtsman who had witnessed a similar operation on a dust cart during his lunch break. The lower platform also provides a form of step when cleaning out the smokebox, tube cleaning, or for other maintenance at the front of the engine. 26 August 1954.

Of course I cannot comment upon what the design may have been like to drive, fire, maintain etc. The various recollections books tend to wax-lyrical about the exploits of Driver.... with No 600.. but we should not forget there were thousands of footplate crew, thousands of trains and millions of miles covered by the engines in the class. For those who require an extra dose of nostalgia, I can do no more than recommend the biography of Bill Hoole and the autobiography of Norman McKillop, both from Ian Allan. And of course the excellent work of the Gresley Society.

Having just observed a single engine in service, but also having seen I think all the preserved examples (including No 60008 at Eastleigh one morning in the spring of 1964 – a definite 'wake-up' sight on the way to school that day), I am certainly not qualified to give a technical appraisal and besides others far more knowledgeable have already done just that - more than once. Hence I will restrict myself to this pictorial tribute, covering all of the class in as many differing poses as possible.

Technical information is gleaned from Yeadon Register No 1 (Irwell Press) and also the RCTS Locomotives of the LNER Part 2A, both are highly recommended works.

Presentation wise, as this is a book based around the BR period I have decided the best approach is to allow for an average of two pages per locomotive in BR service, followed by a short section containing as many suitable LNER images as it was feasible to locate. I hope in this way the appeal of the design is presented to best advantage.

Hector Maxwell

Note: Where possible the name of the photographer has been incorporated into the caption. However as most of the images used come from the 'unlisted' drawers (my words not those of Transport Treasury) this is not always possible. Similarly dates are included where known. Copies of all the photographs in this book are available from The Transport Treasury; if no reference is shown, please order using the page / image number - and of course the book title!

Below: Here we are at Edinburgh Haymarket shed, No 60001 seemingly now ready for service. The fireman (?) is looking back from his side window so it may well be the engine is reversing which would also explain the steam from the whistle just ahead of the chimney.

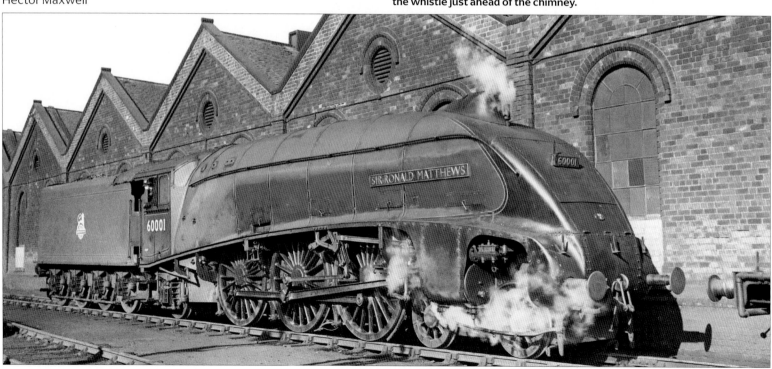

Chronology - A4 Class in Build Date Order

Original number	Entered service	Original name	Final LNER number	BR number	Revised name	Withdrawn
2509	7-9-1935	Silver Link	14	60014	n/a	29-12-1962
2510	21-9-1935	Quicksilver	15	60015	n/a	25-4-1963
2511	5-11-1935	Silver King	16	60016	n/a	19-3-1965
2512	18-12-1935	Silver Fox	17	60017	n/a	20-10-1963
4482	22-12-1936	Golden Eagle	23	60023	n/a	30-10-1964
4483 (585)	26-12-1936	Kingfisher	24	60024	n/a	5-9-1966
4484 (586)	23-1-1937	Falcon	25	60025	n/a	20-10-1963
4485 (587)	20-2-1937	Kestrel	26	60026	Miles Beevor (from Nov 1947)	21-12-1965
4486 (588)	13-3-1937	Merlin	27	60027	n/a	3-9-1965
4487	20-3-1937	Sea Eagle	28	60028	Walter K Whigham (from Oct 1947)	29-12-1962
4488	29-6-1937	Union of South Africa	9	60009	n/a	1-6-1966*
4489	4-5-1937	Woodcock	10	60010	Dominion of Canada (from Jun 1937)	29-5-1965*
4490	25-6-1937	Empire of India	11	60011	n/a	11-5-1964
4491	22-6-1937	Commonwealth of Australia	12	60012	n/a	20-8-1964
4492	27-6-1937	Dominion of New Zealand	13	60013	n/a	18-4-1963
4493	26-7-1937	Woodcock	29	60029	n/a	20-10-1963
4494	12-8-1937	Osprey	3	60003	Andrew K McCosh (from Oct 1942)	29-12-1962
4495	30-8-1937	Great Snipe	30	60030	Golden Fleece (from Sep 1937)	29-12-1962
4496	4-9-1937	Golden Shuttle	8	60008	Dwight D Eisenhower (from Sep 1945)	20-7-1963*
4497	2-10-1937	Golden Plover	31	60031	n/a	29-10-1965

Original Number	Entered Service	Original Name	Final LNER number	BR number	Revised name	Withdrawn
4498	30-10-1937	Sir Nigel Gresley	7	60007	n/a	1-2-1966*
4462	10-12-1937	Great Snipe	30	60030	William Whitelaw (from Jul 1941)	17-7-1966
4463	27-11-1937	Sparrow Hawk	18	60018	n/a	19-6-63
4464	18-12-1937	Bittern	19	60019	n/a	5-9-1966*
4465	8-1-1938	Guillemot	20	60020	n/a	20-3-1964
4466 (605)	26-1-1938	Herring Gull	6	60006	Sir Ralph Wedgwood (from Jan 1944)	3-9-1965
4467	19-2-1938	Wild Swan	21	60021	n/a	20-10-1963
4468	3-3-1938	Mallard	22	60022	n/a	23-4-1963*
4469	30-8-1938	Gadwall	n/a	n/a	Sir Ralph Wedgwood (from Mar 1939)	6-6-1942**
4499	12-4-1938	Pochard	2	60002	Sir Murrough Wilson (from Apr 1939)	12-10-1964
4500	26-4-1938	Garganey	1	60001	Sir Ronald Matthews (from Mar 1939)	12-10-1964
4900	17-5-1938	Gannet	32	60032	n/a	20-10-1963
4901	8-6-1938	Capercaillie	5	60005	Charles H Newton (from Sep 1942) Sir Charles Newton (from Jun 1943)	12-3-1964
4902	28-6-1938	Seagull	33	60033	n/a	29-12-1962
4903	1-7-1938	Peregrine	34	60034	Lord Farringdon (from Mar 1948)	24-8-1966

* Preserved
** Damaged beyond repair in an air raid at York 28/29 April 1942.

No 60001 in action on an unknown working at Naburn swing bridge. Naburn was one of two swing bridges on the east coast main line, the other being at Selby. Naburn was taken out of main line use when the railway was diverted around both in 1983, the original deviation being closed. The bridge structure still survives although the bridge had been 'fixed' in 1967 and in consequence the control cabin was removed.

Above: No 60002 *Sir Murrough Wilson* purportedly in Heaton shed on 16 February 1965. Assuming the date to be correct, also having been withdrawn four months previous. The non-corridor tender will be noted and which in 1948 was also applicable to ten other members of the class. For a withdrawn engine, nameplates are still fitted and the overall external condition is reasonable.

Right: Being turned at Edinburgh Haymarket. From the front painting we can see this was another Gateshead engine and which wording was in addition to the standard BR shed code plate displayed. The engine is being turned by vacuum, a hose connected to the tender brake pipe and with the engine thus providing the power to turn the table itself – far easier than manual effort.

Servicing is clearly in progress here as the covers to the sand boxes are open. Most A4 images show the coupling at the front lifted and placed on the hook itself; unlike other some steam classes on other regions there was no hook under the area of the buffer beam. Notice too at the front there is no steam heat hose. *(Leslie Freeman)*

No 60003

From ground level the impressive lines of the A4 are seen to advantage. As the present writer commented with his personal preference for BR livery for the class, in similar fashion the position of the front numberplate breaks up the otherwise large area of 'smokebox'. No 60003 *Andrew K McCosh* is in charge of the down 'Flying Scotsman' service, at York. On this occasion the front coupling has not been lifted up. The engine name was that of the Chairman of the Locomotive Committee of the LNER and also one of only five directors to serve the company throughout its 25 year existence.

Left Top: No 60003 working a vacuum fitted freight. Even as the top link express engine of the Eastern Region, members of the class were regularly diagrammed for such workings which often included fish traffic. The autobiography of Bill Hoole refers to how, when hearing of the new French railway speed record of 205mph in 1955, Bill was all for 'having a go' with the train they were working. It was left to his fireman to remind Bill that they had freight behind the tender! Amongst the principal classes of express passenger engines from the regions ('Duchess', King', and 'Merchant Navy'), the A4s were the only ones regularly assigned to this type of non-passenger working.

Left Bottom: Late in life at Kings Cross. Still clean but it will be noted electrification warning flashes have been added. Speedo drive just visible coming from the rear left hand driving wheel.

In pristine green livery and with polished buffers, No 60004 *William Whitelaw* is almost ready for work from Edinburgh (Haymarket) on 20 May 1952. At this stage in its life it was yet to have its long guard irons removed and be fitted with a double chimney, AWS and a speed indicator.

Left: Driver Jimmy Swan of Haymarket (left) with No 60004. Jim was a regular A4 man. Note from the die-block the engine is in forward-gear.

Right: In a scene distinctly reminiscent from the 'Elizabethan' film, No 60004 passes Grantshouse on 20 June 1953.

No 60005

NEWCA

Above: No 60005 *Sir Charles Newton* enveloped in both steam and sunshine at Newcastle. This particular example was fitted with a double blastpipe and chimney from the outset and apart from its final year in traffic spent all its time working from Gateshead depot. Whilst we may be understandably impressed with the speed capabilities of the class we should not forget their pulling prowess; Yeadon recounting how in LNER days the engine had run at 75 miles an hour for 25 miles on level track – but with 21 coaches weighing 730 tons.

Right: With whistle sounding, No 60005 bursts back into the sunshine from the 267 yard Penmanshield tunnel near Grantshouse on 31 May 1952. It was here in 1949 that a fire occurred caused by a discarded match or cigarette setting light to a new type of varnish / lacquer on the inside of the carriage corridor. Two coaches were destroyed and there were seven injuries. Twenty- eight years later in 1979 a section of the tunnel collapsed during maintenance resulting in the death of two workmen. This led to the tunnel being abandoned and sealed with a new alignment for the railway to the west of the original.

Cab view at Doncaster in 1953. This was one of four works visits for the engine in that year; one general repair and three deemed as 'non-classified'. Both driver and fireman were provided with upholstered seats and ATC can be seen to be fitted.

Cab side view, fireman's side, similar on all the class. There is a washout plug for the back corner of the firebox and a brass builders plate, of course. Cab doors were fitted but in this view they are seen folded back. The 'R.A.9' designation signified 'Route Availability, with '9' being the most restrictive.

Left: Humble duty for No 60006 at Grantham in charge of a fitted freight. Amongst the top flight express steam locomotives operating on BR, the LNER pacific types were one of the few regularly diagrammed for freight work, often fish trains from the North East coast to the south. This view shows Sir Ralph Wedgwood at Grantham on this type of working.

Far Left: Probably second only to Mallard so far as fame within the class is concerned, this is No 60007 *Sir Nigel Gresley* appropriately named after the designer. the ATC shoe is fitted with a guard ahead to prevent potential damage from the front coupling.

Left: Under repair – location unknown. This is one of Paul Hocquard's wonderful atmospheric shots, we are fortunate he was active with his camera for the final years of the A4's.

Above: On Southern lines. The now preserved (and privately owned by the A4 Locomotive Society) No 60007, repainted in blue as LNER 4498, passing the Baltic siding on the approach to Winchester City on the first day of its two day Southern tour, 3 and 4 June 1967. The trip commenced at Waterloo and ran through to Bournemouth Central and return to Southampton Central behind the A4. 'West Country' No 34023 *Blackmore Vale* was then used to take the train to Salisbury with the A4 making its way light to Salisbury before returning the participants to Waterloo. On the second day, Sir Nigel Gresley ran from Waterloo to Weymouth and return, although banking was provided from Weymouth by No 34087 *145 Squadron* and again from Poole to Bournemouth by No 41320.

No 60008

Left: Another preserved example is No 60008 *Dwight D Eisenhower* which after its BR service had come to an end was cosmetically restored at Doncaster and presented to the National Railroad Museum at Green Bay, Wisconsin, USA. It arrived at its new home in May 1964. Since that time it has been moved twice, in October 1990 for a brief exhibition at Abilene, Kansas, and famously in 2012 as part of 'The Great Gathering' held at the National Railway Museum, York, when all six surviving A4s were gathered together. It has again since returned to Wisconsin. *(George Heiron)*

Below: In charge of 'The Elizabethan' express. The train was introduced in 1953 and so named as a result of the coronation of the new Monarch. It operated in the summer months each way daily and ran non-stop over the 393 miles between Kings Cross and Edinburgh (and vice versa) in 6 hrs 30 mins at an average speed of just over 60mph, at the time the longest scheduled non stop railway journey in the world.

Right: Late in life, 13 May 1961, at Kings Cross with the later BR emblem on the tender and again electrification warning flashes. At this stage No 60008 had just over two years of operational life left. Presumably the height of the coal on the tender has been gauged before leaving Top Shed? (See also view of No 60014 with the 'Northern Rubber Special' headboard later.)

Another named service operated by the class was the Pullman 'Queen of Scots' train: notice how some services had the nameplate at the bottom of the smokebox and on other occasions at the top. Here No 60009 *Union of South Africa* is in early BR blue livery and as yet without any lettering or insignia on the tender awaits its train.

Right: This time at the head of 'The Elizabethan' at Kings Cross. This was the Up service with a late afternoon arrival – see the station clock in the background. Notice the accumulation of oil and debris on the track, this typical of any station end where a steam engine might stand. *(George Heiron)*

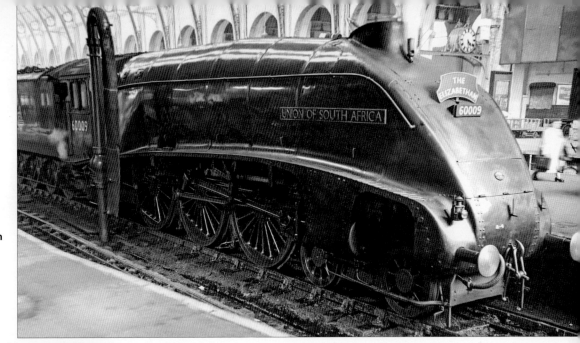

Below: The embellishment on the casing (fitted to this side only) was a rectangular casting of stainless steel depicting a springbok and donated by a Bloemfontein newspaper proprietor. It was affixed on 20 April 1954 at which time the engine was at Doncaster for repair. No 60009 is seen here at Haymarket on 6 May 1956 in company with an A2, which may well be No. 60530 *Sayajirao*.

No 60010

Left: On the previous page we saw No 60009 with the front fairing partly open, here it is in the fully open position and also with the footstep dropped. Careful examination reveals the flattened top to the smokebox door. The location is Haymarket on 22 June 1958.

Right Top: Next we come to No 60010 *Dominion of Canada* working well on the 'Heart of Midlothian' express at Welwyn North; we are told at 2.35 pm, 10 March 1953. This was another named express between Kings Cross and Edinburgh Waverley operating between 1951 and 1968. The shape of the front end casing was intended to serve two purposes; reduce horse power when working at speed, and lift the exhaust clear so as not to impede the drivers view ahead. Both tasks were successfully accomplished – in the case of the latter, notice the exhaust lifted high above the engine. Just visible is the bell, presented to the engine by the Canadian Pacific Railway Company in 1938 located between the whistle and the front of the chimney. This was operated by Bowden cable under the control of the driver. Folklore has it that on one occasion the driver was asked by a young enthusiast to operate the bell as the engine left Kings Cross. This he duly did but then found he could not turn it off. It continued to sound until the train arrived at York when it was possible to turn off the steam supply. It was rendered inoperable soon after and removed in late 1957 consequent upon the fitting of a double chimney.

Right Bottom: Front end detail – double chimney and bell removed. Originally *Woodcock*, when new it had been fitted with nameplates *Buzzard*, but never left the works with these displayed. The *Buzzard* plates were never used and remained in the Doncaster works store for many years.

The final front line service for the class was on the Aberdeen to Glasgow through workings. With just four months of life left, No 60010 is departing for Glasgow from Perth with the 1. 30 pm train, 30 January 1965.

No 60011 Empire *of India* traverses the reverse curves at Grantshouse with the same named train, 'The Heart of Midlothian', illustrated earlier.

Right: Clean condition with later BR emblem on 2 March 1958. Notice that whilst the class type is still painted on the front – as if anyone did not know what an A4 looked like (surely almost the most distinctive of all British loco classes of recent years), the home depot is simply shown by the shed code plate, in this case 64B for Haymarket. No 60011 was renumbered into the BR series as shown on 17 March 1949.

No 60012

Left: Cautiously passing through York on the 'The Elizabethan' (referred to as the non-stop' by railwaymen) on 18 August 1958. York was the approximate half-way point between Kings Cross and Edinburgh in both time and distance and the crew change over – via the corridor tender of course – would take place in this area.

Right Top: In August 1948, extreme weather caused initially flooding and then a breach of the East Coast main line between Berwick and Edinburgh. Such was the tempest that a giant inland lake was formed over a mile long and 28 feet deep, estimated to contain 400 million gallons of water. All this was being held back by a single railway embankment 60 feet in height. In consequence through services to and from the north were diverted via Falahill, Galashiels, Kelso and thence to re-join the main line at Tweedmouth. This was a vastly different route to the East Coast involving fearsome gradients and single line working. Banking was provided although later Driver Jim Swan became the first of several who continued the tradition of the 'non-stop' by managing the route, 408 miles, without stopping. Seen here is another unrecorded occasion when an A4, No 60012 *Commonwealth of Australia* is being assisted, in this case by 'Large Director' No. 62691 *Laird of Balmawhapple*.

Right Bottom: Kings Cross departure. No 60012 has previously arrived with an unreported working and is working back light engine to Top Shed for servicing.

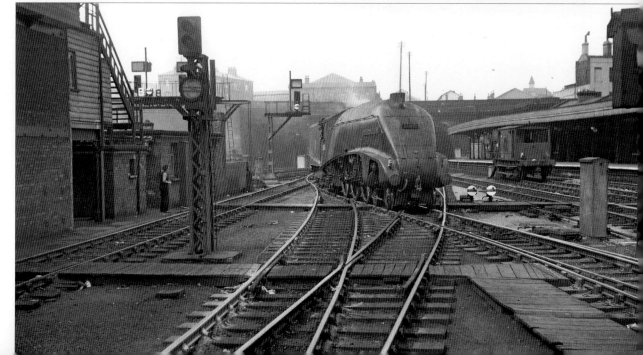

Prepared for service. Originally LNER No 4491, this was one of five engines intended to regularly work the pre-war 'Coronation' service and as such the coats of arms of the named country were painted on to a metal plate fixed to the cab side under the engine number, the engine works plate being resited to the inside of the cab roof. Aside from No 60012, of the other engines so fitted with plates, those on No 60011 and 60013 remained until withdrawal but those on Nos. 60009/10 were removed in 1948 and 1964 respectively. The nameplates for this and several of the other engines bestowed with long names were cast in two parts joined together.

Right Top: No 60013 *Dominion of New Zealand* at Grantham in August 1962, with later BR crest and storm sheet between the cab and the top of the tender. Corridor tender – notice the (grubby) window to the top right at the rear of the tender intended to illuminate the passage way. This particular tender was fitted with Hoffman bearings.

Right Bottom: In charge of the relief 'Flying Scotsman' service near York – the headboard may well be for another working and was being transported back to its home depot, hence the plate is turned to face backwards.

No 60013

Doyen of the class No 60014 *Silver Link*. When renumbered by the LNER in 1946 allocated No 14 which in turn became No 60014. Aside from limited spells at Grantham, No 60014 spent its entire life at Kings Cross where it appears it was a particular favourite and kept in clean condition, that is until labour shortages towards the end of steam rendered this impossible to maintain. The engine is seen waiting to haul the 'Northern Rubber Special'. In the background is sister A4 No. 60004 *William Whitelaw*.

This time at York, light engine on 18 August 1958. As a class the A4s spent a quarter of a century as the lead motive power on the LNER and Eastern Region, as such a longer period than their replacements, the 'Deltic' diesel class.

Not surprisingly No 60014 was chosen for the 'Plant Centenarian' special of 27 September 1953. This was the return of the special from London (Kings Cross) to Leeds, the up journey having been in the hands of LNER 'Atlantics' Nos 251 and 990. *Silver Link* was under the control of Ted Hailstone, another famed Kings Cross man and reached a maximum of 97mph on two separate occasions. In addition the engine surmounted the summit of Stoke Bank at 70mph, this with a trailing load of 410 tons. The burnished buffers will be noted. Sadly this noteworthy and historic engine was cut up at Doncaster in January 1963 just two weeks after being taken out of service.

No 60015

Left: Leaving Copenhagen Tunnel on 11 July 1953, No 60015 *Quicksilver* is working the 9.50 am to Edinburgh. This engine sadly showed the need for longer buffer stocks and an alteration to the original recessed coupling hook which had resulted from a tragic accident during a coupling procedure in July 1936.

Right Top: This time the engine has the 12.30 pm Kings Cross to Newcastle near Brookmans Park on 2 March 1958. Steam from the left hand injector shows the fireman is putting water into the boiler.

Right Bottom: Pending repairs at Doncaster Works on 13 April 1961 in company with K3 No 61927. Yeadon's records indicate a works visit between 19 April and 4 May of that year for a 'Casual Light' repair so it is likely the engine had arrived and was being stored outside with its motion already partly dismantled, before being taken inside the works.

No 60016

Left: No 60016 *Silver King* at Leeds, Neville Hill, on 4 September 1954. In its early days it spent less than two weeks based in London and for the rest of its life was based at the northern depots.

Right: In charge of the 'Flying Scotsman' but without the traditional train headboard, No 60016 eases around the sharp curve at Manors, near Newcastle, on 17 August 1961 and in decidedly grubby condition.

No 60017

Left: A personal favourite, and for no other reason than its supine embellishment, was No 60017 *Silver Fox*. Suitable animal embellishments were fitted to the engine from the outset made from stainless steel and supplied by the steel maker, Samuel Fox & Co Ltd. This was also the engine that featured in the 1954 British Transport Films 'Elizabethan Express'. *(George Heiron)*

Above: LNER livery but BR period, 6 February 1949, two months before being renumbered 60017. The engine is recorded at the slightly unusual location of Cambridge.

Parcels duty for No. 60018 *Sparrow Hawk* at Longniddry on 13 October 1955, with single chimney and AWS is yet to be fitted.

No 60018

Similar duty again with the lead van of Southern origin (No 60018 did work passenger trains as well!). By this stage, 6 July 1958, the double chimney has been fitted, AWS would follow four months later.

The now preserved No 60019 *Bittern*. The engine is in charge of the up 'Flying Scotsman' service at Grantham – the location confirmed by the glass tablet name in the lamp illuminating the position of the water column. Sharp eyed readers will notice one of the headlamps applicable for a 'Class A' working is missing.

No 60019

Late in life and attention to the motion is taking place. Notice the joint in the coupling rod designed to give vertical flexibility and so allow the centre axle to float as necessary. *(Paul Hocquard)*

Turning prior to duty. The flattened shape of the smokebox door shows up well in this image, necessary due to the shape of the streamlined casing. Together with No 60024, these were the final two members of the class remaining in service until 5 September 1966; the first members of the class being withdrawn on 29 December 1962. For Nos 60019 and 60024, their last duties were on the three hour Aberdeen – Glasgow express workings. *(Paul Hocquard)*

Left: No 60020 *Guillemot* at Grantshouse on 20 June 1953 with the 'CTAC Scottish Tours Express'. 'CTAC' stood for the Creative Tourists Agents Conference, a consortium of nine UK travel agents and firms which chartered special trains from 1933-1939 and again from 1945-1968. The headboard colour was polished letters on a pale blue background. Nine coaches make up the load which would not be particularly taxing for an A4 in good condition and with good coal.

Right Top: Certainly no issues with the coal on the tender here and a view also of an A4 with a non-corridor tender. The non-corridor tender fitted engines were still used on the London – Scotland workings but stopped en-route. The 'Talisman' for example called at Newcastle for six minutes allowing time for an engine change and for passengers to stretch their legs.

Right Bottom: Last days, Nos 60020 and 60011 stand nose to nose possibly already out of service. The class served the East Coast main line well and whilst their replacements, the Deltic diesels were at first scorned, they too would develop a following as the years passed. In 1947 it had been planned to rename No 60020 *Dominion of Pakistan* but the politics of the time dictated this was perhaps not entirely suitable.

No 60021

Left: No 60021 *Wild Swan* passing Hornsey on 19 August 1958 – not all inspection covers closed and clipped. Always an English based engine, it moved between Kings Cross, Doncaster and Grantham finally ending up at Peterborough in June 1963, where it spent the final five months of its active life.

Right: Displaying 'The Talisman' headboard at Kings Cross. Notice the foot grips on the inclined framing above and ahead of the outside cylinder.

The most famous of them all No. 60022 *Mallard* on the 'Northern Rubber Special' of 30 September 1961. *Mallard* took the train through from Retford to Blackpool. The return the next day saw No 60022 in company with LMS Compound No 1000 from Blackpool as far as Stansfield Hall.

No 60022

Right Top: In normal everyday service at Hadley Wood. Despite its celebrity status Bill Hoole and others did not particularly rate the engine and considered No 60014 was a far better machine. Whatever, the exploits of 3 July 1938 would ensure No 60022 (4468 as it was then) would gain immortality.

Below: Works and speed record plate detail. The driver is believed to be SR man Bert Hooker.

One could hardly refer to any member of the class as 'mundane' but after No 60022 it is perhaps down to earth with a bit of a bump. Consequently we come to No 60023 *Golden Eagle*, seen at the head of 'The Norseman' train. We only have the year this time, 1958. Six years later this was one of five members of the class taken out of service in 1964.

Signs of modernisation at Hadley Wood on 10 August 1957. No 60023 in charge of a mixed rake of both LNER and BR stock.

BRITISH RAILWAYS
MODERNISATION

WIDENING OF
EAST COAST MAIN LINE
NEW TUNNEL CONSTRUCTION

Left Top: We come now to No 60024 *Kingfisher* and another well-travelled engine certainly in its final years. It is seen here on home-turf at the head of the down 'Flying Scotsman', again at Grantshouse and starting the run down Cockburnspath bank, 20 June 1957. Superb external condition. The new bridge is a replacement for one washed away in the floods of 1948.

Left Bottom: Posed at Eastfield; Driver W McLeod and Fireman G O'Hara. On both sides are plaques of the badge of the then 'HMS Kingfisher' fitted at Haymarket on 21 October 1954. (Driver McLeod featured in the BTF film 'The Elizabethan'.)

Right: On what was now Southern lines and working hard on the steep climb out of Weymouth; banking at the rear provided by Standard Class 5 No 73114. The engine had come south on behalf of the A4 Preservation Society to work 'The A4 Commemorative Rail Tour' although the headboard is perhaps slightly different...? Starting from Waterloo the route was via Southampton and Bournemouth to Weymouth; return Weymouth to Yeovil, and finally Yeovil back to Waterloo.

No 60025

Left: No 60025 *Falcon* at Kings Cross, 19 May 1958. No details as to the train, but the usual 'Class A' headlamps, and coal again well stacked in the tender. Another clean and well presented engine, as well it might be, being based at Top Shed.

Right: Passing Helpston level crossing on a privately sponsored special. *(Paul Hocquard)*

No 60026

Left: Fitted freight duty – unfitted would be really unusual – for No 60026 *Miles Beevor* at Hornsey on 19 August 1958. With no visible exhaust it would appear the engine is stationary; in which case the fireman will ensure it does not release steam from the safety valves and potentially damage the footbridge, the condition of which may already be suspect.

Right Top: Definitely on former LMS territory. No 60026 creates a cloud of steam at Glasgow St Rollox shed on 2 September 1964 whilst waiting to work a Glasgow – Aberdeen express.

Right Bottom: Very close to the end for No 60026 at Perth on 5 August 1966. Condemned from here on 21 December 1965 it was sold for scrap two months later to the Motherwell Machinery & Scrap company but the sale was cancelled and the engine returned to Perth three days before the photograph was taken. Unfortunately it was not for a return to service as by 25 September 1966 it had been towed to Crewe where the three driving wheel sets of No 60026 were exchanged for those on the recently preserved No 60007. The wheels from No 60026 were in better condition. The remains of No 60026 were eventually sold for scrap to Messrs Hughes, of Bolckow, Blyth in September 1967 and No 60026 was no more.

No 60027

BR No 60027 *Merlin* after arrival at Kings Cross; headboard already turned over – unless it had been like that all the time. This was one the class to have four different numbers during its life. Starting off as No 4486, it changed to 588 (but only for five weeks) then No 27 and finally as seen. One of the Eastern Region Pullman services is in the background whilst on the near platform is the detritus of the steam railway, including several end corridor blanks. *(George Heiron)*

Right Top: Final BR condition at Haymarket. The plates on the side are for *HMS Merlin*, a shore establishment, and were fitted in 1946; originally on the cabside but moved as shown in 1948. As well as having four different numbers, the engine had also carried four different names – and all on the same day! This was on 10 August 1944 in the works yard at Doncaster when it was renumbered 1928 *Brigit*, 1931 *Davina*, and 1934 *Bryan*; all to commemorate the birth years of the children of Fitzherbert Wright, a newly appointed LNER director. The changes were made using transfer numbers and applied to the left hand side of the engine only at a time when it was painted in all-over wartime black.

Right Bottom: Near Haymarket, 24 April 1949. The WD in the background is one of those carrying a BR number in the 63xxx series, but was later renumbered 90072 from July 1950. For a time in LNER days the A4 ran with a totally black smokebox carried down in a vertical line to the rear of the cylinders. It was not a paint scheme that worked well for the design.

No 60028

Left: No 60028 *Walter K Whigham* on the non-stop, 'The Elizabethan'. The best A4s were kept for these type of pristine duties with No 60028 clearly highly regarded even as late as 1961. On 8 June that year the Kings Cross shed-master, Peter Townend, was instructed to provide motive power for three Royal workings on the same day – the day of the wedding of the Duke of Kent in York Minster. He had at his disposal English Electric Type 4 and Deltic diesel types, but instead chose steam; Nos 60003 and 60015 for the 'lower orders' but No 60028 for the Queen and entourage. All three performed superbly. Just 18 months later No 60028 was withdrawn and scrapped. *(George Heiron)*

Right Top: Leaving Waverley southbound on 11 July 1953 - next scheduled stop Kings Cross. The grimey V2, No 60949 appears somewhat woebegone but they were a very capable class of engine.

Right Bottom: Extra special non-stop duty or perhaps a visitor on the footplate as well? The presence of the inspector leaning out of the cab window is the clue.

Opposite: No 60028 cautiously making its way south at Hadley Wood during the period work was in progress to increase capacity on the East Coast main line - as part of this work the new tunnel may be seen in the background. The train is not identified although clearly a prestige Pullman working of eight cars some with named roof boards. No 60028 is none too clean but otherwise appears to be in fine fettle with no escaping steam.

Top: Reversing, or waiting to reverse, out of Kings Cross. No 60029 was one of four of the class to carry the experimental liveries of 1948/49 at a time when BR had yet to decide on the final colour scheme for express passenger types. The choices were purple, dark blue (which from contemporary colour images looked well) and finally the standard dark green. Notice too the dropped buckeye coupling on the tender. Water pick-up gear was fitted to all the A4 tenders. *(George Heiron)*

Bottom: Possibly taken on the same occasion, No 60029 has also caught the attention of the young spotter as it makes its way from the station towards Top Shed for servicing. A friend of the present writer recounts how as an 8 year-old, he was sometimes taken to Kings Cross to watch the arrivals and departure, the highlight being when on one occasion he travelled on the footplate of an A4 from the buffer stop to the end of the platform. He admits it was of course in reverse and at slow speed but nevertheless *an experience still recalled many decades later. The British Railways AWS shoe may be seen just behind the front coupling.*

No 60029

No 60030

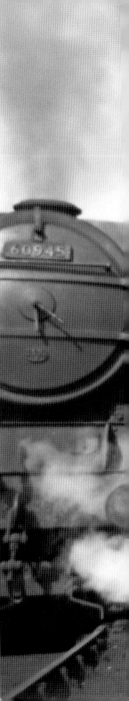

Left Top: No 60030 *Golden Fleece* has charge of 'The Tees-Thames' express. This was a short lived service, 1959-1961 operated between Kings Cross, Middlesbrough and Saltburn. A member of the crew is climbing back on board whilst a solitary spotter seems none too impressed – perhaps he had already seen the same engine several times before. *(George Heiron)*

Left Bottom: Running on the up fast line at Hadley Wood, the new formation with the down line tunnel is on the left. The old bore was 232 yards long, the new one opened in 1959 longer at 384 yards. 18 May 1959.

Right: Edinburgh Haymarket and a rose between two thorns perhaps? Not really as all three were fine engines. On the left we have V2 No 60945, centre is of course No 60030 and on the right A1 No 60150 *Willbrook* dating from 1949 and destined to have the shortest life at 15 years; this compared with the V2 at 22 years and the A4 at 25 years. Incidentally No 60945 was one of the class sent off-region to Swindon for final cutting up. On the front of No 60030 the reverse of the headboard reads, 'Return to DMPS Kings Cross'.

No 60031

Left Top: One of the final survivors of the class (29 December 1965) No 60031 *Golden Plover* with the yellow cab stripe signifying it must not work under the 25kv catenary south of Crewe (although in reality this was hardly ever likely). It is believed to have been recorded on special train duty. Another engine so adorned was No 60027 *Merlin*. *(Paul Hocquard)*

Left Bottom: A few years earlier and in sparkling condition on 'The Elizabethan' non-stop working. The steam issuing is from the fireman's side injector, hopefully pending the water supply being turned on or off, but otherwise not a wisp of escaping steam is seen anywhere.

Right: Steam to spare this time, No 60031 and appearing to be coasting downhill – no location given but probably in Scotland. The fireman is also taking the opportunity for a breather leaning from his window. The image was recorded on 15 August 1957 and the engine retains its single chimney. A double chimney and blastpipe were fitted during a general overhaul at Doncaster early the following year. *(N Fry)*

Left: Kings Cross departure for No 60032 *Gannet* at the head of the down 'Elizabethan', complete with polished coupling, cylinder covers and buffers – possibly a VIP was travelling, 9 August 1954. From the number of observers on the platform this would seem to confirm the special working. (Nowadays probably no one would be allowed near the platform on such an occasion without being searched and their identity confirmed.

Right Top: Another named service, 'The Tees-Tyne Pullman' recorded near to the Welwyn tunnels at 1.40pm, 10 March 1953. Running between Kings Cross and Newcastle and of course behind steam until the A4 class were displaced by diesels, the service operated from 1948 until as late as 1978. By this time air-conditioned stock was becoming standard and Pullman travel in non-air-conditioned stock was also becoming dated, especially as there was the need for an additional supplementary ticket. In the background notice the splitting colour light signal - the days before 'feathers'.

Right Bottom: Crossing Selby swing bridge when this was the course of the East Coast main line. The Selby diversion of the 1980s, constructed partly due to fears of mining subsidence in the area meant the main line took a diversion. Selby though still carries railway track but only that leading to Hull. The structure is also listed.

No 60033

We have seen an A4 on a fitted freight but how about one on an unfitted service? Well all is perhaps not quite as it seems for No 60033 *Seagull*. Yes it is certainly coal wagons behind the tender but only for a very short distance, No 60033 having been purloined at Kings Cross for a shunt move.

Right Top: Fitting 'The Elizabethan' headboard to a sparkling engine at Haymarket and opposite the tool store.

Right Bottom: Passing Craigentinny on the outskirts of Edinburgh with 'The Capitals Limited ' (not to be confused with the similar sounding GWR service). This ER train operated each way between Kings Cross and Aberdeen running non-stop between London and Edinburgh. Again possibly a special day due to the polished buffers. It ran for just three years, 1949 to 1952 and was succeeded by 'The Elizabethan'.

Left Top: The final member of the class to be illustrated in BR condition was No 60034 *Lord Faringdon*. Seen here near Selby. No date or train detail is given but it may well a summer service due to the number of coaches – 13.

Left Bottom: Again 'The Capitals Limited' photographed in July 1949. Carriage roofboards will also be noted, each of these sign written by hand by craftsmen employed by the railway. British Railways and previous to that the LNER, were diverse employers.

We conclude the BR section of this book with the same engine, No 60034, but on vans in Tay Bridge yard; as late as 4 December 1965. No 60034 had another eight months of service remaining.

LNER livery

Left: LNER 4500, later BR No. 60001, likely in early 1939 and just prior to being renamed from *Garganey* to *Sir Ronald Matthews*. The nameplate is covered up and according to Yeadon the cover was subsequently removed without ceremony. Light blue livery with chrome letters and numbers. Full side skirts ahead of the cylinders and part way over the driving wheels.

No 4463 *Sparrow Hawk* leading D49 No 264 *Stirlingshire* away from Waverley on an up express in 1935. Double heading with the class does not seem to have been all that common so might it have simply been a means of transferring one or other engine compared with a light-engine move? The side skirts were removed from this engine in November 1941 to facilitate maintenance and ease of access to the motion.

Left: Head on view of No 2510 *Quicksilver* at Peterborough on 18 October 1936 with a Westinghouse brake test train. (Less than two years later it was with one of these test trains that the world record speed was achieved.) At the time of the photograph the engine was just 13 months old, having already received longer buffers and the engine number painted on the buffer beam.

Above: No 4469 *Sir Ralph Wedgwood* as seen running in March 1939 and thus soon after losing its original Gadwall name. This was the engine bombed in York shed in April 1942 only a few days after having received a general overhaul at Doncaster. Engine including boiler were written off and scrapped but the tender was later repaired and subsequently ran behind an A2/1. The name off No 4469 was also resurrected on to No 4466 (605) subsequently BR No 60006 from March 1944. More than 70 enemy aircraft were involved in the air raid which included the deliberate machine gunning of civilian streets intended to break morale. 92 persons were killed and hundreds injured.

A4's with mixed ownership details but still with LNER numbering at Haymarket. Only one of the pair may be positively identified, No 4 *William Whitelaw*.

Left Top: Identified of course by its bell, this has to be *Dominion of Canada*, No 4489. The train is the 10.00am departure north from Kings Cross to Edinburgh, more famously known as the 'Flying Scotsman' photographed at Craigentinny.

Left Bottom: An excellent sideways view of No 27 *Merlin* sometime after May 1946 and before March 1948; at the latter date the prefix 'E' was temporarily added ahead of the number. The view was taken at Craigentinny carriage sidings and also shows the naval plaques in their original position on the cabside. The side skirting on this engine was removed in late 1941.

Right: No 4492 *Dominion of New Zealand* on the turntable at Haymarket. Rumour has it the side-skirts, especially those ahead of the cylinders, accentuated overheating problems with the inside big-end: BR later adding their garlic 'bombs' which would go off in the event of excess heat being created. Whilst the general shape of the engine did save horsepower at high speed, how much was contributed by the side-skirts is not reported.

No 24 *Kingfisher* leaving a smokescreen, at the request of the photographer perhaps. Scenes such as this were once commonplace, not just the engine that is but the exhaust from the chimney which could be due to a number of additional causes; a dirty fire resulting in incomplete combustion or poor quality coal. With the view taken in the mid to late 1940s either or indeed both could well be the cause.